Kate,
We've never
with your fathe ... *g*
very simple - and ... *—*
years ago. Thank you (see page 114).
In gratitude!
Anthony

CW00972898

Creating A REMARKABLE YOU!

A Simple Guide to Creating a
REMARKABLE Life for Yourself!

by

Anthony McGloin

Grosvenor House
Publishing Limited

Anthony McGloin is hereby identified as author of this
work in accordance with Section 77 of the Copyright, Designs
and Patents Act 1988

The book cover picture is copyright to Anthony McGloin

This book is published by
Grosvenor House Publishing Ltd
28-30 High Street, Guildford, Surrey, GU1 3HY.
www.grosvenorhousepublishing.co.uk

A CIP record for this book
is available from the British Library

ISBN 978-1-908105-22-6

About the Author

Anthony McGloin has invested thousands of hours over many years, learning from the best in the world in the fields of both Business and Personal Development. He runs an award-winning Business with his wife Julie, helping people transform their lives by achieving outstanding success in their business.

But it wasn't always like this.

Life has had its ups and downs and when he needed help, himself, to handle the emotional challenges of a serious accident to one of his children, he looked around for support and guidance.

He found very little available.

So, he decided to learn for himself how to 'grow' as a person - and found surprising strength from within. As he combined his own skills with what he was learning from others, he started to create his own blueprint model for overcoming life's many challenges.

THAT is what you're about to learn in this book.

He is happily married and a very proud Dad. Other rewarding experiences in his life include playing representative sport as well as meeting and working with some of the all-time 'greats', including (at the age of 12) John Lennon, who arranged all the Beatles' autographs for him...and Nelson Mandela, who told Anthony he was an 'inspiration'.

For further help, guidance and inspiration in
both your Business & Personal Life, visit
www.straightforwardsuccess.com

Dictionary Definition
(taken from Merriam-Webster):

re·mark·able
adj \ri-'mär-kə-bəl\

Definition of *REMARKABLE:*
worthy of being or likely to be noticed,
especially as being uncommon or extraordinary

First Known Use of *REMARKABLE*
Circa 1604

Dedicated to:

Nathalie, Claire & Michael.

Babies-turned-children-turned-adults
who make my world a REMARKABLE place.

Contents

Part One

Introduction to
Creating A REMARKABLE YOU!

Being the 'best you can be'

When my 16 year old daughter, Nathalie, was paralysed in a car accident on her way back from school in 1999, there were very few places to turn to for help and support in dealing with the situation. So I found ways myself to overcome the challenges, often finding surprising strength from within.

In the following pages, you'll learn how to access similar strengths within you, to create A REMARKABLE YOU! for yourself!

You'll discover techniques and exercises to help you get through the difficult times and take advantage of the good times. You'll learn how to make the absolute most of your life at ALL times, regardless of your circumstances.

Combining my own life experiences with the proven teachings of personal development experts throughout the ages, this book is for you, regardless of whether you are currently in a 'good' place or a 'bad' place in your life.

All you need is the desire to take control of your life and make the decision to BE more, DO more, HAVE more, CREATE more and GIVE more from now on.

In the weeks immediately following my daughter's accident, I felt compelled to record everything that was happening in a journal. As I wrote about the daily events in the hospital and my accompanying emotions, I discovered for myself how to move forward and my journal eventually evolved into something much greater than just simply a record of my own personal feelings.

The end result is what you're reading now – a practical guide to overcoming life's obstacles and to making the very most of your life.

This is one of 'life's little instruction books' to help you create A REMARKABLE YOU!

A quick personal introduction…

Because we're talking about 'life' here, it's worth you knowing a bit about me and my own life before we get into transforming yours!

First of all, I expect in many ways I'm a bit like you. For the formative years of my life, I had never taken any real time to focus on my future.

In fact, well into adulthood, if someone had asked me what my 'purpose' was in life, I wouldn't really have understood the question, let alone be able to give a true answer. I hadn't really ever thought about it. It had never occurred to me to question why I was put on this planet.

Life's 'Purpose'

You may be thinking exactly the same thing now, as you read this page. After all, have you ever really taken time to consider what you were *meant* to be doing with your life?

The strange thing is that you probably analyse all sorts of other things that you have absolutely no control over: your friends...your partner...the weather...the sports results...the traffic...your work colleagues. Yet, what about the one and only thing that you have TOTAL control over – YOUR OWN life?

The fact is, whether you know it or not, no matter how trivial or magnificent it may be, you DO have a purpose to your life. Maybe you haven't found yours yet, in which case I fully understand. You see, I had been 'wandering around' in my own life for the first 25 years without any real purpose. However, I eventually found my life's purpose on the three days my children – Nathalie, Claire and Michael – were born.

I had become that most cherished of privileges – a parent, a Dad! In those moments, I discovered my purpose: to be the best Dad I could possibly be. Those three days that my children were born were the most exciting days of my life!

Regrettably, an unfulfilling relationship within an unhappy marriage led to a difficult divorce, which resulted in my children growing up hundreds of miles away from me. I sunk into despair, as my role as a Dad became a long distance one.

I thought that being separated from my children was the toughest thing life could throw at me.

My life's purpose became compromised and my whole life became confused. I experienced a potent cocktail of discouragement, anxiety, despair, anger, sadness, self-pity, disenchantment and disappointment.

Even despite an exciting and loving relationship with my wonderful new wife Julie, in many ways my life was largely unfulfilled and unfulfilling. For many years, I floundered and lost my way in life and yet maintained a mask of happiness and positivity to the outside world. This created an anxious conflict between the positive mask on the outside and my true internal feelings.

Then, as I gradually learned how to stop feeling sorry for myself and began to focus on others, I identified a capacity inside of me to inspire and help others achieve their own true potential. This book is the result of that transformation.

It began as the daily journal at my daughter's bedside after her accident, in the early stages of the year she would spend in hospital, learning how to re-build her life through an intensive and often brutal process of physical and mental rehabilitation.

I kept on writing, day after day for the first few weeks in an emotional account of events, feelings and thoughts that explored the full range of the new, unfamiliar world I was experiencing around me. Then one day, I had the privilege to walk alongside my daughter as she pushed her wheelchair, unaided for the first time, from her hospital ward to the canteen, so we could share a drink together.

How proud and inspired I felt on that day! I felt her future calling her forward, towards achievements that have been utterly inspiring and quite REMARKABLE ever since then. She finished school, graduated from University and now, a few years later, is competing at the highest level in the Paralympics sport of Wheelchair Rugby.

My other two children, Claire and Michael have similarly been the source of immense pride and inspiration to me, as all three have grown into wonderful adults, forging REMARKABLE lives of their own.

My purpose has been re-discovered and expanded – to one of discovering and sharing the WONDER in the world!

And guess what?

There really is an abundance of inspiration and wonder in the world. The potential to be REMARKABLE is already inside each and every one of us, just waiting to be discovered.

This book will help you discover it in yourself!

Your REAL strength comes from WITHIN

For most of my early adult life, I had been searching for answers *externally,* from something or somebody ELSE. I was looking *outside* for ways to improve my own life and had never really, myself, taken responsibility to look inwards. I had never really been serious about making things happen.

Instead, I had been lazy, waiting for other people or changing circumstances to show me the way.

Sound familiar?

Then I learned that my true inspiration came from *within*.

The same will apply to YOU – if you let it! Whatever you achieve and whatever obstacles you overcome will come from a strength WITHIN you. You may just need a bit of help to get started, that's all!

That's where this book will help you – providing encouragement for you to discover and release YOUR OWN untapped potential. By completing the simple and liberating exercises contained in these pages, you'll learn the same powerful techniques and lessons I discovered, that helped me overcome my most difficult of challenges.

It's a simple, easy-to-follow guide for anyone seeking improvement in their own life.

This will work for YOU!

If you're ready for growth and increase in your life, this is for you. You'll work through exactly the same principles of success that have helped countless others around the world. They'll work for you if you're already on the road to success. They'll work for you if you're currently uncertain about your future. They'll work for you if you're going through challenges and difficulties of your own.

The exercises each take just 5 minutes to complete and they will help you dramatically improve your life.

How do I know?

Because these very same principles and concepts helped me transform mine!

'Personal Development' has been around for ages – in fact some of the best books on the subject are over 100 years old.

It was something I first really discovered in the mid nineties, in a mesmerising two-hour presentation from a successful South African advertising executive called Mike Lipkin, who fought his way through bipolar depression and back from the brink of despair.

At that time, I was experiencing a depression of my own, brought on by the 'loss' of my children, who were by now living hundreds of miles away. His story ignited the spark of realisation that my own destiny was in my own hands.

Years later, I was introduced to Anthony Robbins, a larger than life personal development 'guru' from America. You may have heard about his events, including his famous 'fire-walk' that helps you overcome the (natural) fear of walking barefoot across burning embers. By doing this, you learn how to use the power of your own mind to overcome other fears and challenges in your life.

So it was for me. I learned how best to deal with the wave of emotions engulfing me at that time in my life and, above all, I discovered how to give myself 'permission' to take back control of my life.

Latterly, I have met and studied many other experts in personal development, including Bob Proctor, Mark Victor Hansen and Michael Beckwith, all of whom have helped me understand the awesome power in each and every one of us – to take control of our life and make the most of it.

However, let's be clear about one thing right at the start: to engage in meaningful Personal Development and to create **A REMARKABLE YOU!** you'll need to step out from your comfort zone and away from the safety of 'the crowd'. You must want to develop for *yourself*, on your own terms.

Yet, have you noticed how difficult that can be?

The vast majority of people nowadays choose to 'march with the masses', stifling their own individuality and staying in a largely unfulfilling comfort zone of *dis*comfort.

However, when you decide to look WITHIN yourself (rather than outside to everyone else) for the answers in your life, you'll discover the incredible power you have WITHIN YOU to improve your own life.

This power remains untapped and unused in most people. The fact is that while growth and development is available for all, only a tiny fraction genuinely commit to maximising their true potential in life. I urge you to be one of the few – to become the best you can be.

It's the birthright of everyone – and that means YOU!

So, I'm inviting you to make a commitment to yourself – one that will supercharge the exercises in this book and make them really work for you!

That commitment is to *BE more, DO more, HAVE more, CREATE more and GIVE more* in your life from this moment onwards.

All it takes is a decision …and the discipline to create the necessary drive to literally transform your life.

Making the most of your Life

Whatever the challenges in your life, there really is only one answer. That is (and I make no apology for repeating it) to find the solutions from WITHIN YOURSELF.

The exercises in this book will help you do just that.

This is YOUR opportunity, regardless of the current circumstances and situations in your life. All you need is to have the DESIRE to be the best you can be.

By the way, if things aren't that great for you at the moment, know that adversity has created a fierce determination to succeed in some of the world's most inspiring and successful people.

It is our duty TO OURSELVES to be the very best we can be. However, it isn't always easy to carry out that duty.

Things happen and emotional baggage gets in the way. Life itself contains no guidebook on how to cope with serious challenges in life. So, I created this one, to help me through my own challenges and to help you with yours.

If it helps just one person ...

>...overcome a difficult challenge in their life
>...find inspiration and excitement for the future
>...treasure a relationship they were taking for granted
>...learn how to make the very most of their life
>...become happier and more successful
>**...it will have been worth every minute.**

<u>**Let that 'one person' be YOU!**</u>

In the next few pages you'll find two separate sections to help you do just that.

- *5 Minutes to A REMARKABLE YOU!*

The A-to-Z of Personal Development, with 26 simple, powerful exercises that take just 5 minutes each, to help you make the most of your life – and be the best you can be!

You'll learn how to take real control of your life and make the CHANGES to transform your future.

Now, isn't that an exciting prospect?

- *Re-building A REMARKABLE YOU!*

Discover the 12 stages of overcoming significant emotional events in your life, to help YOU handle difficult circumstances and emotional trauma, now or any time in the future.

Let's hope you'll never have to use these techniques for yourself. However, if you do – or if someone close to you needs help at any time in their life – they'll prove invaluable!

Part Two

5 Minutes to A REMARKABLE YOU!

The A-Z of Transforming Your Life

Take real control of your life… in these 26 simple exercises.

This is all about YOU. You're about to create a happier, more successful future and a new, **REMARKABLE YOU!**

You'll work through the A-to-Z of emotions, feelings and concepts that fight for supremacy on the battlefield of your mind.

These highly effective exercises will help you take control of the most important areas in your life…just 5 minutes at a time.

This is your fast-track course in Personal Development.

Get Ready!

Firstly, this needs your COMMITMENT and PARTICIPATION, so stop reading this right now! Grab a pen and notepad. You'll need them to get the most out of this section. Go on, stop reading and get that pen and notepad now…!

OK, have you REALLY done that?

Great.

Next, take a look at the A-to-Z list below. You'll be working through each 'letter', completing the 5 minute exercise for each one.

It's important to actually DO these exercises. I know how important this is – because for years, I used to skip through the 'working' parts of books like this, thinking I'd come back to them later. Guess what? It never happened. It was only when I started taking myself and my future seriously that I started doing things like this.

THAT's when I started to see serious benefits.

So, when you start the exercises, take time to think about each one and to write down your answers.

Here's the A-to-Z list you'll be working through:

A – Anger	O – Optimism
B – Belief	P – Purpose
C – Contribution	Q – Questions
D – Depression	R – Relationships
E – Emotions	S – Sense of Humour
F – FEAR	T – Time
G – Goals	U – Uncertainty
H – Health & Happiness	V – Vision
I – Inspiration	W – Wonder
J – Joy	X – X-Rays
K – Kindness	Y – You
L – Life (goes on)	(A REMARKABLE YOU!)
M – 'Major on the major'	Z – Zest (for life)
N – Negativity	

How to complete this process

You may choose to 'skim' read through all the exercises first, before actually working on them. That's OK. However, when you do start working on them properly, start at letter 'A' and complete that exercise before moving on to letter 'B' and completing that exercise. All you need is 5 minutes at a time...

Simply move forward through the alphabet until you've completed all the exercises for all the letters.

These simple 5 minute exercises are designed to help you take back control in key areas of your life. Take them seriously and give them real focus.

Some may seem to cover similar ground. That's because they DO! Some of these concepts are so important that coming at them from a different angle gives a different perspective. Believe in them! Complete them!

<u>They will help you change your life</u>.

Remember, I know this to be true...because they helped me change my own life. They provided the catalyst for my own personal growth and helped me develop in a way that was completely beyond me just a few years ago.

Over the years, I've invested thousands of hours in learning from (and spending invaluable time with) the 'gurus' – the very best 'teachers' in the world – who have helped me pull myself up by my bootstraps and start enjoying life again.

5 Minutes to A REMARKABLE YOU! will do the same for you, regardless of whether you're a personal development 'junkie' or doing something like this for the first time!

In particular, if you're experiencing any form of challenges in your life at present (and let's face it, at some level most of us are) these little exercises will help you overcome those challenges and learn how to enjoy life again.

So, back to your pen and notepad!

The real benefit is in the <u>writing down</u> of your answers! That way, you're telling your brain that it needs to take notice and that you're serious about making improvements. Your brain is more powerful than any computer ever made, so when you direct its focus correctly, it will help you find the answers. You just have to tell yourself that you mean business.

A final (and important) note before you get started

Trying to complete all 26 exercises in one go will be too much at any one time. It would be mentally exhausting! It's much better to take it slow and give yourself the time for real focus. When you've finished, you'll have a valuable A-to-Z of how to improve your life.

N.B. The final exercise (for the letter, Z) is 'ongoing'. To complete it fully will take you much longer than 5 minutes. It may take you 50 years! That's the exciting bit!

It will be a great feeling when you've finished! When you've completed your A-to-Z, you'll have a whole new set of values and the start of a new life!

Starting with 'A', here's to your own personal creation of a new, **REMARKABLE YOU!**

A – Anger

Anger is the most destructive force in your life. When you hold anger in your life, it destroys you, starting from the inside. And, like other negative emotions, the crazy thing is that <u>you're the only one</u> who experiences this negative emotion.

The object of your anger is often completely unaffected and unaware of the negative feelings boiling away inside you. So why put yourself through it in the first place, when the only one who suffers is YOU?

Stand aside and let anger pass you by. When you neutralise your anger – whether it be towards someONE or someTHING – you take back the power from that situation. You regain the control.

Anger takes your positive energy away from you and puts a barrier up between you and the ones you love and the things you enjoy.

And…have you noticed how anger almost always gets you thinking about the past? The fact is you can't do anything about the past – except LEARN from it.

Learn to replace the anger you feel towards negative situations of the past with more positive emotions towards the really important things in your future.

OVER TO YOU FOR...

5 Minutes to A REMARKABLE YOU!- Anger

Anger is a THIEF! This destructive emotion STEALS precious things from you. Think back carefully through your life and make a list of the <u>Top 3 Things</u> you have allowed to be stolen from you, through your anger, in the past.

For each of those 3 occasions, think about how you could have acted differently at the time. How might the outcome have been different if you had been able to maintain control over your anger?

Now, write down one thing that is CURRENTLY making you angry... and that you are in danger of losing, as a result of your 'anger'.

Now, confirm one thing you'll do in the next 24 hours, relating to this current situation, to neutralise your anger and thereby protect yourself from the 'thief' that is called anger.

B – Belief

...in yourself

FACT – You can get through whatever problems exist in your life.

How do I know this is true? Because you're reading this page right now. You're here. You've actually dealt with everything life has thrown at you so far!

You're more than a survivor.

You're a SUCCESS!

Use this fact to create genuine belief in yourself for the future. Congratulate yourself for being strong. Develop the habit of patting yourself on the back and telling yourself you believe in YOU. Actually do it. Get ready to pat yourself on the back in the next few moments. Think of just one thing, anything, that you have <u>ever</u> done that made you feel proud. Now, put your hand over your shoulder and pat yourself on the back for achieving that thing.

STOP READING RIGHT NOW and do it!

It feels a bit weird – but doesn't it feel good too?

You see, when you truly believe in yourself, when you know that you hold the key to your own life, you'll find a conviction that not only supports your belief; it BUILDS your belief and confidence to do other things.

When you have a belief in yourself, <u>YOU</u> become your OWN inspiration. You tell <u>YOURSELF</u> what to do. You no longer have to seek approval from others. You stop allowing other people to decide your future.

This is particularly important if you've fallen into the bad habit of listening to others all the time, waiting for *them* to tell you what *they* think is right for *you*.

YOU are the one who is living your life, so make sure YOU are the one who decides HOW to live it and the direction you take.

It's no good standing in the queue at the Railway Station, waiting for the stranger in front of you to choose your destination for you…or asking for a ticket to nowhere. Trust in yourself and develop a rock solid belief in your decisions!

OVER TO YOU FOR…

5 Minutes to A REMARKABLE YOU!- Belief

What's the MOST IMPORTANT thing you want to achieve in your life? Think about it. Dig deep. Find the TOP priority in your life.

What were you put on this earth to achieve?

Whatever it is, write it down NOW.

Then close your eyes and picture yourself having achieved it. Throw yourself fully into this exercise. Enjoy the moment and imagine what it looks like to have <u>achieved it</u>. What it feels like to have <u>achieved it</u>. What are the sounds you're hearing when you've <u>achieved it</u>?

Immerse yourself in the scenario of this achievement. Let your imagination run wild with feelings of success, pride and achievement!

Now, open your eyes and capture those moments. Quickly, while they're still vivid, write down the top 3 feelings that came to you in your imagination.

Doesn't that feel GREAT?

The world's greatest achievers and inventors have proved beyond doubt that 'if you can hold it in your Mind, you can hold it in your Hands'.

Well, you've just held your Belief in your Mind, which means you can hold it in your Hands...and make it a reality.

You just have to believe you can do it.

C – Contribution

'The greatest reward is not in receiving but in giving'.

How true that saying is. Yet the funny thing is that if you haven't experienced the feeling for yourself, you probably have no idea what it really means.

When you learn the concept of contributing and giving to others, you'll start experiencing how great it really feels.

When you contribute to, or help, others and when you are genuinely interested in other people's well-being, you'll surprise yourself at just how much better this will make YOU feel as well.

The amazing thing is that when you start doing this, you'll also start attracting into your own life those people who will contribute to you. It works with all the important things in life, including Love, Happiness and, yes, Money.

Whenever you feel desperate about your own situation, go out and actively look for ways to help others. There's a whole world of abundance out there, with people just waiting to 'give'. Join them.

It will work wonders.

OVER TO YOU FOR...

5 Minutes to A REMARKABLE YOU!- Contribution

Think of just one person or organisation that you can help this week. Make a commitment to help them, with absolutely no expectation of reward in return.

Write down the name of that person or organisation and precisely what you will give to them. It may be giving Money to Charity or volunteering your Time to someone less fortunate than you. It may be as simple as phoning a relative and giving them the gift of a 'hello'.

Whatever it is, do it just ONCE a day for the next week. Then see if you can ever stop! The more you give, the better you'll feel and (in a remarkable way that is difficult to explain) when you really do contribute to others with no thought of getting anything in return, you'll find that people start to give to you in lots of ways too. It's called the Law of Reciprocity. The world really is an abundant source of resources. Live a Life of Abundance!

D – Depression

Depression comes in various guises. In my own life, it started when I first experienced the 'loss' of my children, when I found myself living hundreds of miles away from them.

Ironically, it was this depression that led to my interest in personal achievement, development and motivation. I began to realise that we all have an immense capacity and power to heal ourselves from within.

It's interesting that looking back to when I was at my lowest ebb in life, my doctor did not prescribe anti-depressant drugs for me. Perhaps he determined that my depression was not severe or that I was strong enough to deal with it.

What I know is that when I went into that doctor's surgery, I *thought* I was in desperate need of medication.

However, when I came out of that same building just a few minutes later, I felt stronger for having been given the confidence that I could beat the negativity on my own, without the help of drugs.

It gave me a strength that I had not felt before, yet one that was clearly within me all the time.

Depression plays its role perfectly. It depresses you. It suppresses you. It stops you thinking your way clearly through situations. It holds down all of your positive energy and emotions. It blocks everything.

In that environment, your negative emotions are given full rein and your demons are given the space to run riot.

In my case, on the turn of a friendly, empowering comment from my doctor, I realised that I had the power – in myself – to fight back.

You can, too.

Use the following exercise to prove it to yourself!

OVER TO YOU FOR...

5 Minutes to A REMARKABLE YOU!- Depression

Fight depression from within!

Take a moment to think of the one thing that depresses you most in your life at this time. Take a piece of paper and write the 'name' of this thing in the middle at the top of the paper.

Next draw a line vertically down the centre of the page forming two columns underneath the word. Write the words 'How this depresses me and makes me feel' at the top of the left hand column – and the words 'how I will overcome this feeling' at the top of the right hand column.

Now simply fill in the two columns. For every negative feeling you list in the left hand column, write down exactly how you will fight this negative feeling and overcome it.

The cruel thing about depression is that it sometimes makes you feel as if you want to wallow in self pity.

The fact is, however, that at the outset, you can make a choice to be strong or to be weak.

CHOOSE TO BE STRONG. Know you can do this.

Use this technique for any part of your life where you need to fight back and gain control of your emotions.

E – Emotions

When a significant emotional event affects your life, it's important to accept that your emotions will experience incredible upheaval. It happens with positive and negative emotions alike. Your heart leaps skywards with wonderful news and plunges into the deepest abyss with catastrophic news.

When you first fall in love, your emotions sing to the heavens in joy. Similarly, negative emotions can take you to the depths of the ocean of your being.

Know, however, that you CAN control your emotions. Your thoughts create your feelings (which in turn, lead to your actions). Your feelings and emotions therefore are the result of your thoughts – and YOU are the only one who can think your thoughts.

That means you can learn to control them, too. It will not always be easy but you must welcome constructive, positive thoughts and you must let the destructive ones pass by.

An expert in this field is Bob Proctor and if you are interested in this topic I urge you to research his teaching on this.

Be aware, however, that controlling your thoughts isn't always that easy! That's because your mind may be filled with negativity that becomes overwhelming. You may feel dominated by Anger and Fear, directed at various people and various things. These emotions sap energy from you and regularly leave you feeling helpless.

However, as you emerge from the dark times, you'll find yourself replacing those negative emotions with positive ones (for example, increased <u>love</u> for your 'loved ones' and increased <u>enthusiasm</u> for more positive times ahead).

What would happen to your emotions if you replaced your Anger with Love and replaced your Fear with Enthusiasm? Have you noticed how much clearer your thoughts are when you feel 'positive'? Negative emotions are shrouded in mist, while positive ones gain crystal clarity.

Start controlling your thoughts and you'll start controlling your emotions. Your life will become clearer and you'll feel much more in control.

OVER TO YOU FOR...

5 Minutes to A REMARKABLE YOU!- Emotions

What are your top 3 negative emotions?

Write them down, together with one significant negative thing that each of these negative emotions has led to.

For example, if Fear of failure is on your list, perhaps the one thing this has led to is a reluctance to try anything new – which has led to stagnation in your life.

Can you see how these negative emotions affect not only your thoughts but the things you do (as a result of your thoughts).

So, let's regain control of your emotions!

For each of those 3 negative emotions, write down the OPPOSITE <u>positive</u> emotion.

Now imagine the difference in your life when you replace your negative emotions with positive, empowering ones. Imagine the difference in your life when you train yourself to focus on these positive emotions.

Imagine how much more enjoyable your life can be!

From now on, whenever you start thinking negative emotions, stop yourself and ask yourself this question: 'What is the opposite of this negative emotion? What can I do right now, to start feeling good about this situation?'

Start focusing on the positive thoughts and feelings in your life and allow them time to breathe and grow.

It will work wonders!

F – FEAR

In the previous exercise on Emotions, Fear was identified as a possible negative emotion.

Do you know what the word FEAR really stands for?
    False
    Expectations
    Appearing
    Real.

This means that the fear of something is usually much worse than the thing itself.

Learn to use this to your advantage with the following exercise!

OVER TO YOU FOR...

5 Minutes to A REMARKABLE YOU!- Fear

What is the one thing that you fear the most in your life? Whatever it is, stop reading and write it down now. (By the way, the mere act of writing this 'fear' down will strip it of some of its power over you).

The 'opposite' of FEAR is HOPE – powerful and compelling 'HOPE', so we'll use HOPE to combat and overcome your fear.

Learn to expect that things will be fine and you'll develop an almost uncanny knack of making those good things happen. (For more about this, look into the many books and films about the Law of Attraction).

Now, next to what you've written down as your biggest fear, write down the HOPE that you have for a better outcome in that situation. Allow this HOPE to compete head on with your fear and defeat it.

It's a scientific fact that your brain thinks you want more of what you focus on, so it's your choice: will you focus on your Fear – with all its debilitating consequences or will you choose instead to focus on and embrace your HOPE, focusing on a better future?

Learn to dismiss your fears by expanding your HOPES and DREAMS. Create a crystal clear vision of what you will achieve in a future full of HOPE.

Start right now focusing on your HOPES and ambitions for the future!

G – Goals

Growth and Increase is the natural state of every living person. It's also the law of nature that when you stop growing, you start to die.

For example, did you know that some statistics indicate that the average time from retirement to death can be as little as 2 years?

How can this be so?

It's because when people retire, they often decide that they've reached the end of the line. They think that as far as life is concerned, 'that's it'. In those cases, without new, exciting goals for the later stages in life, it's like saying 'my terminal decline has started'.

What nonsense! You're as young as you think you are.

Whatever age you are, be on the constant lookout for growth and increase. Find the ways to create new ambitions and desires. There's no need to follow the masses...or other people's plans for you. Create your own Goals, plot your own course and set sail!

The painter Michelangelo first said, 'People don't fail because they aim too high and miss but because they aim too low and hit'. It's as true now as it was back then.

Set Goals in every area of your life and use the acronym – **SMART** – to help you complete them.

When you set a SMART Goal, it stands for:

> **S**pecific – what are you specifically going to do?
> **M**easurable – how will you measure your progress?
> **A**chievable – make it achievable.
> **R**esults-Focused – what longer term results will this goal bring?
> **T**imescale – Set actual dates for completion of your goal.

Bestselling author Brian Tracy says that writing Goals down increases your chances of success by 1000%! That's a pretty impressive increase in your chances of success.

Making your Goals SMART stacks the odds even more in your favour! So, let's get this simple, proven method of achievement working for you straight away.

OVER TO YOU FOR...

5 Minutes to A REMARKABLE YOU!- Goals

Give yourself time to think about what you really want to achieve in the next 90 days. Write down your Top 3 Personal Goals and make each of them SMART.

Remember what SMART stands for:

> *S-pecific*
> *M-easurable*
> *A-chievable*
> *R-esults-Focused*
> *T-imescaled*

Having done that, it's now much easier to create the discipline to make them happen.

Laminate these 3 SMART Goals and take them with you everywhere.

See how your focus on your Goals will help you find ways to make them happen.

Go for it!

H – Health & Happiness

How important is it for you to be Healthy and Happy?

Do you know that people have cured themselves of life-threatening diseases through laughter and by watching comedy films?

We all know the benefits of keeping our bodies healthy but not so many people pay the same attention to their minds.

If you feed your body with junk food, it's accepted that your health will suffer. So what do you think happens when you feed your mind a diet of depressing news and bad intentions?

To be able to help yourself and others, you must look after your mental AND physical health and well being – that means both Body AND Mind.

Feed your body with the right nourishment and it will serve you well. Do the SAME with your mind, too. It also requires a healthy diet!

The superfoods for your mind include positive ambitions and positive challenges. Tests have shown that we use only 5% of our mental capacity in our lives, so there's plenty available. You just have to choose to use it!

Read the best books that will help you develop and grow as a person. Listen to personal development programs.

Keeping your body healthy and your mind alert and happy will prepare you for all those good times ahead as well as any challenging times that require extra reserves of stamina and fitness…of both mind AND body.

OVER TO YOU FOR…

5 Minutes to A REMARKABLE YOU!-Happy and Healthy

You use at least 17 facial muscles when you smile. So, go on, give yourself a mental and physical workout by smiling at 10 people today.

Start now by finding somebody you can smile at in the next 5 minutes. Notice how infectious a smile can be – and how good it makes you feel.

It may even lead to a 'Happy Ever Laughter'!

I – Inspiration

Inspiration comes in variety of guises. You can choose to be inspired…or you can choose to be inspiring.

Or both.

The BBC News presenter George Alagiah tells a story about when he was reporting from a war-torn part of the world and he met a woman called Fatima in a remote village. As they were filming, she looked up at him from where she was on the ground and said 'I am so sorry that I am so poor'

Can you imagine that?

Here was a woman with such humility that she was actually apologising for being one of the poorest people in the world.

In that moment, she was an inspiration to us all.

We all have people by whom we are inspired. I have had the privilege of meeting some hugely inspiring people, including Nelson Mandela, who exuded humility and inspiration in the gentle way of those for whom it comes naturally. This remarkable man, who inspired countless millions himself, told ME that I was an inspiration, too.

How humbling! His mere words served to inspire me.

We ALL have the capacity to inspire and it's our duty to make the most of the talents in our own lives. It's also our responsibility to allow our own 'light to shine', to inspire others to do the same.

When you do so and when you are THE BEST you can be, you can consider that you are helping people like Fatima, the woman who was so sorry that she was so poor.

So from now on, whenever you slacken in an important endeavour; whenever you start to give up too early; whenever you under-perform; whenever you fail to grasp the nettle of achievement, remember Fatima – and make a commitment to be the BEST YOU CAN BE.

We all owe it to Fatima and the millions like her around the world to inspire everyone we meet and encourage them to do the same.

Learn to be an inspiration to everyone you know!

OVER TO YOU FOR...

5 Minutes to A REMARKABLE YOU!- Inspiration

Make a list of the 3 most recent things in which you 'fell short' of your own expectations.

In each case, identify the common thread – the ONE thing that let you down most in that endeavour.

What you're looking for here is a personal characteristic of yours that frequently lets you down.

When you have identified it, write down a commitment for the next 7 days to prove to yourself that you can inspire yourself to be better in that area.

For example, if you threw some litter down in the street, you may identify a 'couldn't care less' attitude. If so, you could volunteer to help clean a local hospital car park.

Be harsh on yourself and see it through.

Let your light shine to inspire yourself and others!

Be serious with this commitment – and follow it through.

J – Joy

Look for the good in all things. Find ways every day to smile and be happy. Look for joy and happiness wherever and whenever you can, no matter how difficult your life may seem at times.

It could be as simple as having fun with your pet dog or cat for 5 minutes. If you're currently experiencing sadness in your life for whatever reason, prepare for fun and joy to come back into your life.

Welcome joy and happiness back into your life NOW!

Learn how to smile again!

It can be a turning point, just finding out that you CAN smile again.

Search for your own joy and keep it alive, even if sometimes you feel you don't know how it will ever re-emerge.

Be open to the emotion of joy. It will come from unexpected sources when you invite it in.

OVER TO YOU FOR...

5 Minutes to A REMARKABLE YOU!- Joy

Write down ONE thing that has brought you great joy in your life. For example, it may be a relationship, an event or an achievement. Whatever it was, identify it.

Now describe how it made you feel.

How does it make you feel NOW, thinking back to it?

Capture that feeling and describe it, together with a specific activity you will engage in during the next 24 hours…to feel that same joyful emotion again.

Write it down!

Remember, the mere act of writing it down will tell your brain that it's important to you and will put your senses on alert for ways to experience it.

Be on the constant lookout for ways to bring joy into your own life – and the lives of others!

K – Kindness

This is a wonderful principle: Reach out to help others and accept their hand when they reach out to help you.

Sometimes the smallest gesture will mean the most to you.

(See examples of how the kindness of 'strangers' can mean so much in the three stories involving well-known celebrities at the end of this book).

Remember, giving is far more rewarding than receiving.

Who can YOU reach out to?

Who can you be kind to, today?

OVER TO YOU FOR...

5 Minutes to A REMARKABLE YOU!- Kindness

Decide on the person you're going to be kind to today. Charity begins at home so let's start with someone you love.

What treat can you organise for them, simply by going a little bit out of your way? Make it as little or as big as you like – and it need not cost you any money.

For example, imagine the delight when your children wake up to find their names written outside in the snow? Or the help you give to someone crossing the road?

Spend 5 minutes coming up with the idea that will mean a great deal to someone.

Maybe it's a little note, or perhaps a more elaborate arrangement to provide something you just know they'll love.

Organising it will be fun for you and your true reward will be in the delight of the loved one who receives it.

This little exercise will prove to you again just how much fun can be had in giving, rather than receiving.

L – Life (goes on)

No matter how catastrophic a situation may be to you, the fact is that other people in the world may remain completely unaffected, unaware of what has happened.

Your own life may have been turned upside down, yet a neighbour just a few yards away may be celebrating wonderful news that very same day.

Difficult as it may be to accept when tragedy strikes, it is your *interpretation* of the situation that determines how you feel and how you respond.

Whatever your personal circumstances, you must have a 'compelling future'. This is the basis of goal-setting and the foundation for human growth and achievement. It allows you to see beyond a tragedy or catastrophe and continue moving forward towards that future.

If you are experiencing hardship of any kind, without Dreams and Ambitions it can seem like the end of the world. At best, when you have nothing to strive for, nor aim at, you'll wander aimlessly through life accepting whatever 'comes your way'.

Medically and scientifically, it has been shown that those who heal most quickly from physical or emotional injury are those who maintain an optimistic view of their future. They have a compelling reason to get better. These are not just 'positive thinkers'. They combine their positive thinking with positive ACTION because they have something to look forward to.

What is your own 'compelling future'? If you don't have one, the real danger is that you follow someone else's path, which will take you to where THEY want to go, not where YOU want to go. Life 'goes on'. Make sure YOUR life goes on in the right direction – the one you've intended.

OVER TO YOU FOR...

5 Minutes to A REMARKABLE YOU!- Life (goes on)

What IS your compelling future? What is the one thing that will keep you on track when times are good and help you get back on track when times are tough?

It's your life – start building it in the next 5 minutes.

If you know your compelling future, write it down now, describing it as clearly as you can. If you don't have a clear picture of your future, start creating it now!

M – 'Major on the major'

Major on the major things in life – not the minor things.

In the workings of the human mind, it's been proven that you spend most time DOING the things that you spend most time THINKING about.

So, it's worth making sure you're thinking about the things that really matter to you.

OVER TO YOU FOR...

5 Minutes to A REMARKABLE YOU!-
Major on the Major

Let's make sure you KNOW what the major things are in your life!

Consider the 5 areas of your life shown below and for each one, write down the one thing that is most important to you in that area.

1. *Family*
2. *Health*
3. *Career*
4. *Financial*
5. *Social*

Now, ask yourself how much time you have given to those 5 things in the last week – and most importantly, set a goal for doing something positive for each one in the coming week.

Performed regularly, this simple technique will to help you identify how well you are managing your 'major' priorities.

N – Negativity

Have you noticed how most people focus on the negative?

You only have to watch the news or read the newspaper to have your mind crammed full of negativity. This diet of negativity can have only one result – more negativity.

No-one sits down and purposefully makes a decision to become a negative person. However, how many people do you know where negativity has just become a 'way of life'?

Perhaps this even applies to you!

Negativity is something that you inherit from the past (often unwittingly) and that inhibits your future. Left anchored in your sub-conscious mind, these negative thoughts can cause untold damage and have a huge negative impact on your life.

Imagine how liberating it will be to break free from this habit of negativity!

Most people are experts in negativity. They know exactly what they DON'T want or like. Worse still, they pass their negative habit on to their children, habitually telling them NOT to do something, rather than encouraging them to DO something.

This negativity is a pandemic of biblical proportions – learned and passed down over generations! So, how, exactly, are you supposed to overturn negative habits of many lifetimes? The answer is in the law of physics! For every negative, there is a positive. So, you can either focus on the negative or the positive. It's as simple as that. It really is. It's your choice.

It takes just as much effort to focus on a problem as it does to focus on the solution. Here's a good example. Let's say, you're always late to work and you always ask yourself '*Why am I always late for work?*'

The focus on the negative (being late) will confirm in your mind that being late is the 'norm' and you'll find ways to achieve it more often!

However, if you ask yourself one day '*what do I need to do to get to work EARLY tomorrow?*' then your focus will be on providing the positive solution.

The answer to your question will be very different.

OVER TO YOU FOR...

5 Minutes to A REMARKABLE YOU!- Negativity

Let's turn the tables on negativity! Let's make things POSITIVE, starting NOW.

CREATING A REMARKABLE YOU!

Firstly, make a conscious effort to take the word 'not' out of your vocabulary for the next 24 hours. Just see the impact it has on the way you talk and think! You'll surprise yourself at just how many times you use this word in your daily life.

When you get rid of the 'not' word (think of it as 'untangling the nots'), you'll find you start adopting a much more positive approach to your life.

Next, list your 3 worst, most negative habits – the things you'd most like to get rid of.

For each one, make a written commitment to replace ('old negative habit X') by its opposite (positive habit 'Y').

For example:

'I now commit to replace my old negative habit of arriving at work 3 minutes late...with my new positive habit of always arriving 10 minutes early. I'll chat positively to my colleagues and start the day off in a positive, calm manner. To achieve this, from now on, I commit to catching the earlier bus – every day!'

See how easy it is!

Once you've made the commitment, all you need to do is DO IT!

All it takes is awareness of the negative habit and a discipline and commitment to make the necessary changes.

The 'Law of Vacuum' states that when you get rid of something of LOW VALUE in your life, you must replace it with something else of HIGHER VALUE.

So, be on the lookout all the time for ways to add higher value to your life!

O – Optimism

The antidote for negativity!

Have you ever noticed the refreshing optimism of those people who succeed in life? It's even more refreshing when you see people succeed in life in the face of seemingly insurmountable odds.

There's a story about a prisoner of war who was kept in solitary confinement for many years. He kept his mind active by 'mentally' playing his favourite sport – golf – every day in his prison cell.

He played his imaginary game of golf over and over again in his mind, looking forward to the day he would be able to do so for real again, physically, when he got back home. When he was eventually released after many years, he was actually a BETTER golfer than before his imprisonment. That's because he had been 'playing' every day! He KNEW he would be released and his unyielding optimism kept both his mind and body alert.

Thomas Edison's discovery of the electric light is another great example of optimism. When asked by a reporter how he felt about all the failures he experienced on the way to discovering the electric light, he replied that he had never failed once. Each time he 'failed', he simply considered it one step closer to success. He viewed as a success what others perceived as failures – and it's just as well he did!

The mind is the most powerful thing known to man...and optimism is a state of mind. It provides the environment for fantastic achievements to take place in your life.

You are, indeed, what you think – and you can make the CHOICE to think optimistic thoughts!

OVER TO YOU FOR...

5 Minutes to A REMARKABLE YOU!- Optimism

Take 3 important areas in your life (for example, 'Health' or 'Fitness') and write down a realistic, optimistic Goal for improvement for each one in the next month.

How much better will your life be, when you have achieved that improvement? Find out by making your Goal SMART and then acting on it!

P – Purpose

It's been said that the two most important days of your life are the day you were born and the day you find out your 'Purpose – the reason WHY you were born.

So, what is the Purpose of <u>your</u> life?

It's not a question most people give any thought to.

What do you enjoy doing most? What makes you feel most alive? What do you want to be remembered for?

When you discover your Purpose, you truly can start doing everything 'on purpose'. It gives you a real focus for your life and will act as the fuel in your life tank. It will help you get up ready for each day, determined to make the most of it.

Yet, most people go through life without a purpose.

If you have never considered this question before, now would be a great time to start by asking yourself:

What are you here to accomplish?

When you find the answer, you'll want to enjoy each and every day in the pursuit of that purpose.

How much time do you currently waste watching meaningless TV or engaging in idle gossip, simply because you have 'nothing better to do'?

The truth is, you DO have something better to do! If you don't know what it is, here's how to start finding out!

OVER TO YOU FOR...

5 Minutes to A REMARKABLE YOU!- Purpose

Write down the answers to these 5 key questions:

1. *If everything ended tomorrow, what would you regret most? What have you left 'undone' in your life?*
2. *What do YOU want to be admired for?*
3. *What will your legacy be – What do you want to have created in life?*
4. *How would you like your friends to describe you?*
5. *What makes you feel GOOD?*

You see, it's not that difficult. You just have to start asking yourself the right questions.

Q – Questions

As you'll have seen in the previous exercise, the right questions are the first stage to finding the right answers.

The incredible thing is that the answers to most of your questions already lie within you. However, you may have to dig deep to find them. That's why most people don't bother. It's just too much like hard work.

Einstein famously said that THINKING is the most difficult work known to Man, which, he added, is why so few people engage in it!

THINK about the right questions to find the right answers. If you keep asking yourself why everything is dreadful, then you'll find lots of answers to that question. You'll find more things that are dreadful.

By turning that situation on its head and asking yourself 'how can I make it better?' you're on the road to the solution. Get your powerful computer-brain to start working for you, finding the answers to what you *do* want, rather than against you, finding more of what you *don't* want.

Just because you're stuck inside a box called 'Unhappy' at the moment, does not mean you have to stay there.

There's another box called 'Happy' – and all you need to do is find your way from one box to the other.

You simply need to find the right directions…by asking the right questions!

So let's start this process right now.

OVER TO YOU FOR…

5 Minutes to A REMARKABLE YOU!- Questions

Pick one situation in your life that makes you 'unhappy' at the moment.

Now ask yourself: What's needed to make you feel 'happy' about that situation? Use your answers to write down 3 things that need to change for you to start feeling good about it.

Then start making those changes.

R – Relationships

What relationship do you value most in your life? How do you treat that person? How do you nurture that relationship?

Now ask yourself this question: What can you do in the next 3 days to make it (even) better?

Identify the relationships that will support you and nourish you mentally, both in good times and in challenging times. Let the negative relationships go. They become a drain on your health, your outlook and your future.

Focus on the relationships that matter.

You can never tell what is going to happen in the future to the people you love. So, invest time with them right now. You love them anyway, so you'll both enjoy the experience.

Live in the present. It's called the 'present' because it is just that – a gift.

Give your important relationships this gift of being in the 'present'. If a relationship lasts for 100 years, you'll have had a great time for those 100 years. If for any reason, the time is cut short, you'll have lived life with that person to the full.

You just can't ask more than that. Live life in the Present with the ones you love – NOW!

OVER TO YOU FOR...

<u>*5 Minutes to A REMARKABLE YOU!- Relationships*</u>

Who is the most important person in your life? When was the last time you told them how much they mean to you?

Identify the top 3 things that you're going to do within the next 24 hours to improve this relationship, to make that person feel really special.

If your relationship is already good, how can you make it even better? If it's not as good as you want it to be, what needs to happen to improve it?

Make SMART Goals and as soon as you've written them down, start doing them!

S – Sense of Humour

Whatever you're going through, good times or not-so-good times, it's vital to keep a sense of humour.

When you can laugh in the face of adversity, it helps your whole being. Find time for humour and fun whenever possible, giving light relief to your mind and in so doing recharging your batteries, ready to deal with the more serious situations in life.

Think of your mind as an electrical circuit, using energy to deal with your day-to-day life. When you're dealing with difficult circumstances, you're draining the reserves of mental energy.

Similarly, humour, smiles and laughter replenish those reserves with a new supply of energy and well being.

Laughter has been known to heal serious illness. Use it to fill your mental tank with mental energy.

OVER TO YOU FOR...

5 Minutes to A REMARKABLE YOU!- *Sense of Humour*

Think of one situation that frustrates you at the moment – perhaps for example, something annoying at work or home.

Now, write down just one light-hearted aspect of that situation, that puts it into a more balanced perspective.

You see, it isn't the <u>situation</u> itself that distresses you. It is the impact it has on you that causes the upset. It's <u>your interpretation</u> of any given situation that affects how you feel about it.

That means you can control how you feel about any situation...just by thinking about it differently!

Many of those little irritations in life have light-hearted sides to them. When you find that humour, suddenly, your irritation reduces. In fact, often it disappears completely.

Look for the things that make you smile and enjoy those moments, looking for ways to share your laughter with other people. It is a great medicine.

Take it often!

T – Time

Beware the saying 'Time is the Healer'. It's NOT true!

YOU are the healer

In many cases of emotional distress, your brain will not allow you to focus fully on the enormity of a situation until it knows you can handle it. Until then, it may allow you only glimpses of the true situation.

When you prove to yourself that you are ready to handle it, your brain will give you the strength and ability to do so. When you are strong enough to see the whole picture, it will allow you to see it.

It depends on YOU, not time.

Yet, have you noticed how some people *never* emerge from a tragedy? They live in the past, focused on what they have LOST, never allowing themselves to move forward, to what they might FIND to replace it. This makes it impossible to live enthusiastically in the present, let alone believe ambitiously in the future.

It is YOU, not 'Time' that is the healer.

So, when your life is affected by a significant emotional event, it is vital to accept the changes that have happened and accept the new circumstances of your new reality.

Your Life has not stopped. It has CHANGED (even though that change may be significant). How well and how quickly you RESPOND to that change defines your future.

As your circumstances change, so you must adapt, creating new ambitions and new Goals. These may be different to your previous ones but <u>must</u> be focused on finding ways to increase and grow from your new circumstances.

It is truly the difference between those that view a tragedy as the start of their own decline and those that accept their new (changed) circumstances... and move forward to REMARKABLE achievements.

Take the Time to enjoy life, whatever life has in store for you.

OVER TO YOU FOR...

<u>*5 Minutes to A REMARKABLE YOU!-*</u>
<u>*Time (is NOT the healer)*</u>

You can't change Time.

It's what you DO with it that is important.

Think back 10 years. Remember how your life was back then and write down the Top 3 most noticeable ways you have changed as a person in the last 10 years.

Now think FORWARD 10 years from now.

DESCRIBE the person you want to BECOME in the next 10 years and write down the Top 3 things you will have changed in yourself, to become that person.

Which is more exciting – reviewing the past (that you can do nothing about) or dreaming about the future (with its endless possibilities)?

The next 10 years will tick on by, 86,400 seconds every day. Use each day to make your life fulfilling!

U – Uncertainty

Certainty is one of the basic human needs.

Uncertainty about the future can wear you down quicker than almost anything else. It is a debilitating adversary and wrestles control away from you.

In times of stress and anxiety, it is vitally important to create stability in the key areas of your life.

It's important to identify and confirm those certainties that exist in your life. These are the foundations that will help your new growth.

For the important things in your life, you must gain Clarity and Certainty.

Know where you're going. Know why you're going there. Know when you get there.

Whenever you're uncertain of something important, invest time in finding out the facts. When you have knowledge of the facts, you can make the right decisions and take the right course of action.

OVER TO YOU FOR...

5 Minutes to A REMARKABLE YOU!- Uncertainty

What are you currently most <u>uncertain</u> about in your life?

(If this is difficult to pinpoint, think about what area you're most <u>uncomfortable</u> about. The two are probably linked).

Now, having identified this 'uncertainty', write down the top priority, starting TODAY, that must happen for you to re-gain control of this situation.

As with previous exercises, make these actions SMART and start working on them to create your human need for 'certainty'.

Take control of your life by replacing uncertainty with certainty.

It's a simple way to transform your confidence.

V – Vision

An inspiring personal Vision helps you look beyond the difficulties of the present moment and draws you forward towards REMARKABLE achievements.

Mark Victor Hansen (co-author with Jack Canfield of the inspiring Chicken Soup for the Soul books) says that Big Goals get Big Results...and that No Goals get No Results!

It's the same with your Vision.

Establishing a Vision sets your personal objective for success in life. It forms the framework for your ethics, ambition, and goals. It will challenge, motivate and guide you – and inspire those around you.

So, if you haven't got a Vision, no wonder you might be feeling a bit flat!

Open your mind to the importance of having a meaningful Vision of where you're going in your life.

Your Vision defines you and is closely linked to your Purpose in life. People who have neither have no real destination and therefore travel the road of life according to other people's whims and desires.

Let's invest 5 minutes in your Vision for your future!

OVER TO YOU FOR...

5 Minutes to A REMARKABLE YOU!- Vision

Here's how to start create your own compelling Vision:

Break all your boundaries and inspire yourself with a Vision of how GREAT your life can be. Give yourself permission to really dream, without limitation.

> *A great Vision will be:*
> *- Connected to your Purpose*
> *- Your long-term Legacy (so it's not just about YOU)*
> *- General, yet concise and clear*
> *- Focused on a better future.*

For example, the vision of an oncologist may be 'the eradication of cancer'. Alternatively, a musician may choose 'worldwide happiness through music'

In less than 10 words, come up with what YOU want to help achieve in your lifetime. When you've finished, read it out loud. How good does that make you feel?

W – Wonder

When you find 'wonderful' things in the world you become inspired and excited in ways that are sometimes difficult to describe.

Yet few people actively search for these 'wonderful' things.

Imagine how your life will be transformed when you search for and find more 'wonder' in your life?

How much better will your life become when you look for the good in every little thing and share that 'wonder' with others?

Imagine how different your approach to life will be!

Imagine how many more people will be attracted to you and want to be around you.

When you look for the wonder in the world, the world becomes a wonderful place.

OVER TO YOU FOR...

5 Minutes to A REMARKABLE YOU!- Wonder

Where is the 'wonder' in your own life at this moment?

To help you start focusing on this, think about the single most wonderful thing that has ever happened to you in your life up to now.

What is it? Write it down and describe how it made you feel when it happened.

Now go to www.wonderfulnewsnetwork.com – an interactive social media website created specifically to share the 'wonder' in the world. See how many people you can inspire with your story – and how you can be inspired by the wonderful news in the lives of others.

Be on the lookout for wonderful things and acknowledge how they make you feel.

Then find more!

X – X-Rays

X-rays penetrate matter where light cannot pass.

However even X rays cannot show your Soul, your Spirit, your Self – whatever it is at the deepest core of <u>you</u>.

No one has an X-ray picture of what makes you tick, of what makes you get back up when you fall down.

So, if it can't be X-rayed, it can't be 'broken'.

In this next exercise, you're going to look inside of you and find out what really makes YOU tick.

OVER TO YOU FOR...

<u>5 Minutes to A REMARKABLE YOU!- X-Rays</u>

To find out the most important thing about YOU (that remains invisible, even to X-Rays) ask yourself this question:

What is your TOP strength, the one that has, above all else, been the basis of the successes you have achieved up to now? What has helped you achieve everything you're proud of in your life?

Dig deep to reach your emotions and truly find out what constitutes your REMARKABLE YOU!

Take some time to be clear about this. You're looking for the one thing that has helped you most in your life.

Got it?

Great. Now write it down, so you can focus on it.

You have a multitude of similar inner strengths

When you find them, write them down and display them so you see them every day.

You see, there are the things about you that no X-Ray can see – and that can't ever be broken. Remind yourself daily of these strengths – and build upon them.

Y – You (A REMARKABLE YOU!)

'You' are what these exercises are all about.

The biggest obstacle to you fulfilling your potential and achieving success in your life is…YOU!

You can Be more, Do more, Have more, Create more and Give more.

MUCH more!

You just have to truly want and believe you can do it.

> Believe that you can **Succeed.**
> Believe that you can **achieve your Goals.**
> Believe in your **Vision.**
> Believe you can **Inspire.**
> Believe you deserve the **Good life.**
> Believe you will get through challenging times and **emerge stronger on the other side.**

Be clear about what you want. Remember, if you <u>don't know</u> what you want, it's very difficult to find it.

Define the things you DO want – and then set SMART Goals to achieve them.

Remember to congratulate yourself along the way (even if it's just a pat on the back) as you achieve your milestones.

Enjoy your journey as well as the destination.

The great thing about 'you' is that you can CHANGE 'you'.

If you don't like something about you, it's likely others will find it unattractive too. So, change it! You're the only one who can change you. And you're the only one you can change.

Let go of all those negative self doubts and replace them with self belief.

Invest in You.

'You' are an individual. The only person stopping YOU from becoming *A REMARKABLE YOU!* is...YOU.

That means the ONE PERSON who can make you REMARKABLE is also...YOU!

If the people you associate with are holding you back, find new people who inspire you! Find people who excite you and challenge you. Make new friends who will pull you forward.

Invest in YOUR future.

Achieve your goals and fulfil your own true potential.

OVER TO YOU FOR...

5 Minutes to A REMARKABLE YOU!-
You (A REMARKABLE YOU!)

In the previous exercises, you've been working through various aspects of your life. Now is the time to bring it all together in an at-a-glance list of 'YOUR Top 10'.

Write down the answers to these questions:

1. *What do you want most in life?*
2. *What is your life's purpose? Why are you here?*
3. *What is your exciting Vision for your future?*
4. *What Goal is the one that means the most to you?*
5. *What ONE thing do you most need to change about you?*
6. *Why do you want to change?*
7. *What drives you? What one thing motivates you most?*
8. *What legacy will you leave behind for others?*
9. *What is your greatest passion?*
10. *What makes you most happy in your life?*

Now you know 'you' – you're ready to go out and have fun with your life, with the final letter in the alphabet!

Z – Zest (for life)

Since records began, those who have succeeded most in life are those who have had the biggest vision for the future – *regardless of their current circumstance.*

They have that 'zest for life'.

That's what you're about to create in yours. You're going to find out what really excites you!

This final letter of the *A-to-Z of A REMARKABLE YOU!* is about your **future** and is arguably the most important letter of all.

There's a story about a teenager called John Goddard, sometimes referred to as the 'real life Indiana Jones'. When he was 15, he overheard a conversation between his parents and a family friend. The friend said he wished they were 15 again, like John, so they could have achieved some really important Goals in their life.

That comment inspired John and he immediately started to create a list of his 101 'Life Goals' (which eventually grew into over 400)! He achieved them all, including climbing mountains, exploring the world's largest rivers, flying planes, living with tribal groups around the world, holding a variety of world records and speaking a multitude of languages.

He discovered a real ZEST for life!

So are you up for a similar challenge?

Here goes…

OVER TO YOU FOR…

<u>*5 Minutes to A REMARKABLE YOU!-*</u>
<u>*ZEST (FOR LIFE)*</u>

This last exercise will take more than 5 minutes to complete! It may even take a lifetime!

*For now, though, your 5 minute exercise is simple – to choose your <u>**Top 3**</u> most important things that you want to accomplish in your life. These are your WORLD CLASS Goals…your most important ones – your <u>**Top 3 Life Goals**</u>*

Become really emotionally connected to this last exercise. Your life Goals will define you, excite you and inspire you.

When you've written down your Top 3 Life Goals, get your diary out and allocate the time in the next few days to enjoy coming up with the other 98 Goals

(Yes – that's right – and by the way, of course, you don't have to stop at 101).

This may take you a few minutes to complete…a few hours…or a few days. However long it takes…JUST DO IT!

Yes – you may find it difficult.

Yes, you may think that you have 'dried up' after the first few. However, <u>persevere</u> – and have fun planning your exciting future!

Once you've completed your list, guess what? You'll have a clear direction and purpose for your life. What's more, you'll be planning your life based on what YOU want and the things that excite YOU and make you happy. What a brilliant concept – life on your own terms and with your own Goals!

So, when you have your list of Goals, Plan them by making them SMART (Specific, Measurable, Achievable, Results-focused and Time-scaled).

Above all, make them time-scaled, by confirming actual DATES by when you will complete them.

THEN...start doing them!

You will have created a lifetime of excitement and fun to look forward to and the chances are you'll add many more to your list in the years to come!

This will be 'work in progress' for the rest of your life!

By deciding on the Goals, you will have planned something really special. Then, it's up to you to have fun achieving them!

For the rest of your life, you will be truly creating your new **REMARKABLE YOU!**

Part Three

Re-building A REMARKABLE YOU!

*The 12 Stages to Help you Overcome the
Serious Challenges in your Life*

This next section is particularly relevant for anyone experiencing significant emotional difficulties or traumatic circumstances in their life. (If, thankfully, that doesn't include you, then think if there's someone else close to you who may benefit from reading this).

You see, when you're confronted by highly charged emotional distress, you're likely to feel alone. In most cases, very few other people will have had *first-hand experience* of exactly what you're going through.

You often don't know how to feel or what to expect.

In dealing with the major emotional challenges in my own life, I realised that there had been a set pattern of distinct 'stages' each time. It was also apparent that I had created a simple blueprint 'model' for working through each stage.

Most important of all, I found this model worked in a variety of situations – and for other people as well!

So, the following 12 stages of **Re-building A REMARKABLE YOU!** provide that blueprint, to help you overcome 'emotional trauma' or any significant challenges that affect you personally, deeply and emotionally.

The next few pages will help you understand the stages and identify the emotions that may surface with them. They offer help in navigating that difficult journey and suggest ways forward, to overcome your challenges.

It is intended to give you help, encouragement and guidance as well as to ignite the power inside of you to emerge stronger and better equipped to deal with your changed circumstances ...and to re-build A REMARKABLE YOU! If you are prepared to welcome a 'shining light' back into your life, let these few pages help you find the switch to turn on that light.

N.B. This is not a medical 'white paper' proven after years of medical research. However, in many ways the principles are even more relevant, working as they have for me, in my own life. I hope they prove to be similarly valuable for you, in yours.

Stage 1 – Overwhelm

When you first experience or become aware of a tragic event in your life, expect immediate panic and mental shock to overwhelm you.

Accept that this is normal.

You probably won't be able to think straight. There's just so much happening and so much to do. Everything attacks your mind at once.

You feel overwhelmed as your mind attempts to take in what has happened.

Depending on the enormity of the situation, your mind may ration the amount of information it allows you to focus on at any one time. It may allow you only glimpses of the situation, before 'shutting you down'.

This is to protect you and will help you deal with things, bit by bit. Any more would be too much to take in at this time. Stress is like a glass of water. If your stress is high, it's as if your cup is full to the brim and anything, even the merest drop, will cause it to overflow.

Know that this is happening and accept it.

It's just part of the first stage that you'll need to experience.

It WILL get better. Your mind is a powerful computer and when it finds the best way forward, it will guide you.

Stage 2 – Learn the Facts

As soon as you possibly can, learn the facts. Find out the information that will give you the true assessment of the true situation.

Take this information in and process it as carefully as you can. Find out what needs to happen and what you need to do to make it happen.

This will be difficult because your distraught emotions will dominate your mind. However, the facts of the situation will be there, even though they may be hidden under your immediate emotions. You'll probably have to dig deep to gain control and the knowledge of the true facts will help you do that.

As you gain this knowledge, you'll feel more in control. The initial facts may overwhelm you but at least you will know them.

You may then experience a period of apparent calm, where you begin to understand the reality of the new situation.

However this *calm before the storm* may be replaced quickly by a return to an emotional turmoil. When this happens, accept it as a stepping stone to the future, not the dead end street of how things will always be.

Once you confirm the facts, it's important to process them. You'll need to gain absolute clarity and this won't come naturally. You'll need to be strong.

Find out what's needed by asking yourself these four questions:

- *What has happened?*
- *What does this mean?*
- *What else do I need to know?*
- *What are the priorities – what must I do first?*

Once you focus on these questions, they will lead to answers which will give you clarity of purpose and clarity of direction.

Expect your brain's automatic pilot to gain control and to give you direction in the form of your 'gut feel' or intuition. Listen to it and act upon it.

Stage 3 – Control & Plan

The 'responsible person' in you takes over. This may be 'spouse' or 'parent' or 'friend', dependent upon your situation. It will be different for different people in different circumstances.

Dig deep to find that responsible person within you to take control.

Knowing the facts, let the responsible person in you decide on what is needed and then plan what is needed.

In normal life, you are ten times more likely to complete activities when you write them down. It's even more important to do this in this pressure cauldron of your emotional distress.

Make sure you do this – <u>write down what's needed</u>.

Even though writing things down logically in this phase may be extraordinarily difficult, it will be invaluable later on because you will be able to work through the plan (sometimes on automatic pilot) when you know what to do.

Be prepared for shock and panic to return (as they probably will) and know you can re-gain your emotional control by understanding precisely what is needed – and then by taking the necessary action. If you feel unable to do this on your own, find someone to help you.

Even in these early stages, find out what's needed in the longer term and start working backwards. No matter how difficult this is, you will find that the fear of what is to come is always worse than the actual thing itself.

So confront what is needed and write it out, prioritising what is most important. Write down what needs to happen, step-by-step. Include timescales for everything. It will help you gain control of the situation and give you back some of the 'power' you feel you have lost.

Once your list is complete, you'll be ready to start working on it.

Know that you are moving forward by doing this.

Stage 4 – Take Action

Having decided what needs to be done and having written it down, you'll now need to start working through the plan so that the important things get done – in the right order.

It's as simple as that.

Start at the beginning of the plan you have written down and work through the list, step by step.

Stage 5 – Get Support

Decide who you can trust and enrol their support, being aware that this may not be as easy as it seems.

You're looking for non-negotiable TRUST – the person or people upon whom you can rely unconditionally for help and support.

Find them quickly, because you'll need their support throughout this whole situation.

In some cases, this support will be required long term, so make sure you choose the right people – people you can trust unequivocally.

Although it will be disappointing if it happens, don't be surprised when people close to you – even family members – let you down. This will happen because everyone else in this situation is only a peripheral player – they don't understand what YOU are feeling.

Only YOU know what you are feeling.

Others may offer you advice and take decisions from *their* perspective of what is right for you. However, their way of dealing with things may not be right for YOU. They may not be able to differentiate from what THEY

THINK you need and what YOU REALLY need to move forward.

Choose your support carefully and lay out the rules, telling them clearly how you want them to support you.

Get their agreement to play by your rules and then move forward knowing that you are not alone.

Stage 6 – Protect Yourself

In dangerous situations, who should you protect first? You – or the people you love and cherish?

The answer is YOU.

Until you, yourself, are protected you can't protect others.

It's the same principle as in emergency procedures in airplanes. If you're a parent, you must don YOUR oxygen masks first BEFORE attending to your children.

That way, you are better equipped to help them.

So, now, you must do whatever is needed to protect yourself – first.

Once you have protected yourself, you'll be able to better protect the ones you love.

Accept that understanding the enormity of a tragedy may overwhelm you and that your brain may continue to protect you throughout this situation by allowing you just glimpses of the true magnitude of the situation.

As your brain apportions those amounts, bit by bit, so you can handle them and move forward, step-by-step, without being overwhelmed.

Each time, you'll be building your strength.

If your brain doesn't do this automatically for you, protect yourself by understanding that you can't handle everything at once. That is precisely why you've written down your plan of action. Allow that plan to be your guide, focusing on individual priorities one at a time.

Once again, trust your intuition to help you. Trust yourself, because you are the person who knows you best.

Stage 7 – Protect & Inspire Others

In life, giving is far more rewarding than receiving. People may dispute this in today's society but it's the truth.

A life of abundance (of sharing and giving) will always create a more fulfilled existence compared to a life of scarcity (hoarding) and keeping things for oneself.

It's the same when confronted with traumatic or tragic circumstances.

After first protecting yourself, look for opportunities to protect your loved ones affected by the event.

There will even be ways that you can inspire them. This may not be immediately noticeable on the outside but will provide valuable strength to them sub-consciously.

This has two real benefits. Firstly, it will help them. Secondly, as you help others, you will be helping yourself to be inspired…by you.

Again, you'll need to dig deep to access the reserves of strength that lie within you – and you may surprise yourself with just how strong you can be.

The confidence you'll gain for yourself from inspiring others will be immeasurable.

Stage 8 – Temporary Collapse

Just as you think you're gaining control, be ready for the dark shadows to re-appear.

It may happen often.

Be ready for those occasions when you collapse exhausted, both physically and mentally.

Each time it happens, KNOW it is temporary.

Your mental and emotional muscles will have never before been exercised like this, so expect them, initially, to be weak.

You must train them to be strong.

It takes 21 times to establish new habits, so there will be times when your habits are not yet formed and you feel like you're falling back.

When that happens, persevere! Know that you're moving forward all the time.

You may not yet know exactly what that future holds but these temporary feelings of collapse will reduce as you move forward. The 'bad' days will be replaced by 'good' days. It doesn't happen immediately...but it DOES happen.

Accept your moments of weakness as your mind's way of temporarily re-grouping its resources, ready to restore and fight back to rebuild A REMARKABLE YOU!

Be aware of what your mind and body is telling you and act accordingly. For example, if you feel tired and weary, find time to sleep. Sleep can be a great refuge – and every time you wake up, you're one step further forward.

Stage 9 – Restore your Strength

Do whatever is needed to regain your strength – and in certain circumstances, that will include being selfish!

Your strength WILL be needed, that's for certain. It will be needed for you and your loved ones.

Every time you restore yourself to strength, you're building that strength and building the habit of doing so.

Your objective is to create new strength, so that it becomes natural and habitual.

So, set aside time for yourself.

Don't be tricked into thinking you have to be strong for 'everyone'. In this step, you just have to be strong for YOURSELF.

Sometimes your strength will be evident in simple words or a loving remark. Other times, it will be in your thoughts.

You'll only be able to do this by regaining your own strength, ready to draw on those hidden reserves.

Do whatever you need to restore you strength and congratulate yourself every time you display it.

Stage 10 – Embrace the new Reality

Whatever has happened, it's vital to accept that it *has* happened.

Guard against those unwelcome inner voices and thoughts that will try to question what could have been done to avoid what has happened. Such thoughts are now unhelpful.

Wasting valuable focus and energy by trying to turn back the clock serves no purpose. The truth is that the past is exactly that – past! It has gone and will not return.

The sooner you accept the new reality, the sooner you will be able to move forward and build a compelling new vision for the future.

However, you're only human and you may continue to hear those little voices of despair. When you do, create louder, stronger voices of the new reality – and the new vision for your life.

Your new situation and circumstances are the new reality.

That is where you future lies.

How well you respond to your changed circumstances and how well you embrace the new reality will define and determine your life from now on.

Stage 11 – Rebuild your Vision

You can't change what has happened. You can only deal with today and plan for tomorrow.

If you have no plans and no vision for the future, you will flounder, without direction.

As a human being, you have an in-built mechanism that looks to move forward. Acceptance of this fact is vitally important.

If you choose to reject your new circumstances, they will defeat you.

When you choose to accept them and embrace them, you'll find you're on the road to your compelling future.

Remind yourself repeatedly that life has not stopped.

It has just changed.

The sooner you can create a new vision for yourself in your new circumstances, the sooner you can move towards it and make it happen.

The human instinct is to move 'away from pain' and 'towards pleasure'. Yet, if you focus on your 'pain', it slows your speed away from it.

Focus on the 'pleasure' – your VISION.

As you build your new Vision, it acts like a magnet, pulling you further away from the 'pain' and accelerating your progress towards the future 'pleasure'.

Stage 12 – Travel your New Road

It's time for action!

Travelling your New Road is the final stage in helping you re-build A REMARKABLE YOU!

By the time you get to this last stage, you've come a long way!

Now with your Vision established, you have a new direction and a new road to travel, as you re-build A REMARKABLE YOU!

Some years ago, an article by the late Jim Rohn inspired me. The article was called 'Walking a New Road' and over the years, I created my own version, adding to it and changing it often, so that the words became highly meaningful and personal to me. They are shown below and I hope reading them inspires you to create something similar for yourself:

Today I'm Travelling my New Road

I'm now taking control of my future with a commitment to my personal development and to constant and never–ending improvement of 'me'.

I now realise that just small amounts of positive change in key areas of my life all add up every day... and make a huge difference to my future.

I'm transforming my life with ongoing improvement in my Focus, Commitment, Clarity, Confidence, Ambition, Strength, Thoughts, Feelings, Direction, Actions, Determination, Honesty, Congruency, Thoughts ...and my Discipline.

My Thoughts... lead to my Feelings... which, in turn, lead to my Actions

So, from today, I'm Thinking the right Thoughts. I'm Learning the right Disciplines, and Making the right Choices

My future has always been up to me. Today I commit fully to that principle. **My future is absolutely up to me – and me alone!**

I've replaced Blame, Excuses and Denial with Ownership, Accountability and Responsibility.

I'm on my way.

I know that it's not necessary to do extra-ordinary things to achieve extra-ordinary results and I'm making the simple changes necessary to Travel my New Road.

My few, new, daily disciplines will very quickly multiply up and create a huge difference in my life.

I commit to Being more, Doing more, Having more, Creating more and Giving more in my Life.

Every day in every way, I am stronger in mind, fitter in body, happier in life and more successful in business.

I'm starting out travelling my Brand New Road.

Welcome to the NEW ME.

There you have it – my own personal Call to Action to travel my New Road.

Now, it's time for YOU to Travel <u>your</u> New Road.

It may be a different road to the one you originally envisaged but the important thing is that it is YOUR road.

You've chosen your future Destination and it's there, waiting to be reached!

All you need to do is start travelling your new road.

Your future beckons, pulling you forward to a life where you're in control of your life and you set the highest example for others to follow.

You CAN do this. You really can. Starting NOW!

Enjoy the journey!

Part Four

The Kindness of REMARKABLE Strangers!

Billy Connolly; Sir Paul McCartney;
I'm Sorry I Haven't a Clue!

'You can have *anything in the world you want if you'll just help enough other people get what they want…' (Zig Ziglar)*

Some people will be very aware of the help and support they gave to my daughter (and me) after her accident.

Others probably have no idea that their seemingly small contribution created a huge impact and were highly significant in helping us all piece our lives together.

These include the people identified in the following three stories.

These stories are included here as great examples of 'kindness' and as an endorsement of the famous quote shown above by Zig Ziglar.

Billy Connolly

Soon after my daughter's accident my wife and I were due to see the comedian Billy Connolly. This had been booked some time before but I was no longer interested in going.

However, Nathalie was excited at the thought of us going. She said he was her favourite comedian!

My journal entries from the time take up the story as follows:

My mind races – would she like us to get his autograph?

"Could you? Yes PLEASE!" she says.

Would you like me to get him to phone you?

"Yes, Yes YES!" she says.

So I set my mind to work. How can I do that?

I have never even met him and have no obvious way of contacting him. However, I leave messages everywhere I can and eventually speak to one of his entourage. His manager, I think.

Brilliant!

Billy Connolly has agreed to meet us afterwards.

On the night, it's a good show but I'm tired and feel out of place at a comedy event. But he HAS agreed to meet us.

That's great!

When we do meet him afterwards at the stage door, we find him a genuinely nice guy. There's a small group of fans waiting for him and he calls out "where are the people with the daughter who's had an accident?"

He asks if we mind waiting till the end.

When it's just Julie and me, he asks about Nathalie, with obvious genuine concern. I ask him if he could possibly sign his autograph for her. I've bought a card for the purpose and he replies "OF COURSE I will".

The printed card says 'Keep Smiling' and he thinks carefully before writing: 'Dear Nathalie. Keep on keeping on. Thinking about you. Billy Connolly'.

I ask him for one more favour – and he agrees to phone her in hospital. What a treat that will be for her!

The truth is, when I first learned from Nathalie that she actually LIKED Billy Connolly, I was a bit shocked. After all, my little daughter…liking that vulgar humour?

After tonight, however, I'm delighted she does. I like him too.

Mission accomplished!

I speak to Nathalie and tell her to expect a call from 'Billy'. She's delighted but almost embarrassed, saying she won't know what to say to him!

'Billy' DOES phone a few days later! It causes real excitement with the nurses and cheers Nathalie up no end.

I wonder if he knows just how much it has lifted her spirits and how much it means to her (and me).

P.S. Nearly two years later, Billy Connolly was performing in Bournemouth and I made a point of going to see him again. I arrived early and saw him as he arrived.

"<u>Mister</u> Connolly!" I called to him.

Dressed in my business suit, I'm sure I looked like an official of some kind and he seemed somewhat concerned as I approached him, purposefully and obviously with a reason to speak to him.

I called out a loud "Thank you" – and he visibly relaxed!

I asked him if he remembered speaking to my daughter all that time ago. He did, recalling the situation and asking after her. He asked me to send his love to her. It was a display of extra-ordinary sensitivity from someone who must meet all sorts of people all over the world.

Thank you Billy Connolly, you're a Top Man!

Sir Paul McCartney

My children inherited my love of The Beatles.

I had grown up just a short walk from John Lennon's house and my best friend actually lived next door to him! I remember playing football in his garden, hearing the Beatles' guitar sounds as they 'jammed' next door.

One time, I crept through the fence in the garden and went up to the big door that was the Lennon mansion. I knocked on the door expecting to be met by the maid, only to come face-to-face with a big black mop-top of Beatle hair. At 12 years old, I was standing right in front of John Lennon himself!

"Hello Mr Lennon", I said, timidly. "May I have your autograph, please?" John signed his name on the back of an envelope (which I still have to this day) and then said that the 'others' were coming the next day and would I like all of them all to sign a photograph?

"Oh yes please", I said, "Thank you!"

The next day, I walked around through the main gate (the hole in the garden seemed so passé by now) and collected my prized possession. What a treat...and of course a great story to recount to my children, as soon as they were old enough to identify any Beatles song!

So, with stories like these and regular viewings of the cartoon film, Yellow Submarine, my three children became Beatles Fans.

Shortly after Nathalie's accident, I became aware of the publication of the book, The Beatles Anthology. In a moment of inspiration, I set myself the goal of getting her a signed copy for Christmas.

I didn't have a clue how I'd do it. I just knew I would.

Back to my journal entries to take up the story:

It's now November 1999, just two months after Nathalie's accident, and I attend a Business trade show in London. My own rehabilitation into the outside world has been hesitant over the last few weeks and I find it difficult to find any real interest in things that previously have been important to me. Everything seems so shallow and insignificant.

As I walk around the show, an event that for many years has been the highlight of my social calendar, I notice how banal and superficial everything appears. However, I have a purpose for my visit today and I visit the display stand for the city of Liverpool in the hope of finding someone who might know a way of contacting The Beatles.

Alas, I draw a blank.

However, it's still a great idea and, based on the statistic that you're 'only ever 6 people away from contacting anyone in the world', I tell a number of people of my intentions.

One of these is someone I've known for a few years. His name is Peter Moss. He's always been very friendly and I've always enjoyed the occasions I've spent in his company. He's one of life's genuine people and runs the UK destination marketing for Miami, Florida. They always have a major presence at the show.

I chance upon Peter outside his stand at the show. I explain that I'm looking for a way to surprise my daughter by getting an autographed copy of the new Beatles book...and he immediately offers to help.

My heart fills with joy and gratitude.

You see, Peter is the father of Kate Moss (the Model) who asks her friend, Stella McCartney (the Designer), to ask her father, Sir Paul (The Beatle) to sign a copy of the new Beatles book for my daughter.

For the next few weeks, Peter and I liaise to turn my goal into a reality and Nathalie's treasured present arrives a few days before Christmas 1999.

It's a signed copy of The Beatles Anthology, with a handwritten note and smiley face inside from Sir Paul, himself, sending his love with best wishes 'from your friend, Paul'.

It is a fantastic surprise present for Nathalie and means so much to me. And it all started with someone (Peter Moss) going out of his way to offer his help and support.

After Christmas, although Nathalie and I wrote Thank You notes to all concerned, I wonder if they really ever knew the impact their thoughtfulness brought to our family that Christmas.

I'm Sorry I Haven't a Clue!

It didn't stop there.

Another person who went out of his way with kindness to help a 'stranger' was the British script writer, comedian and raconteur Barry Cryer.

Like Billy Connolly and Sir Paul McCartney, he had never met any of us before, yet he, too, fulfilled a promise he made to me during a chance meeting.

He was part of the team from the very funny, typically British radio comedy series called 'I'm Sorry I Haven't a Clue'. (Part of the show involved a nonsensical and hilarious game called Mornington Crescent. It's a family favourite of ours).

I met Barry in a hotel, where he was the after-dinner Guest Speaker at an event I was attending. I asked if he would be able to get his fellow celebrities on the show to send their best wishes to Nathalie in hospital.

He duly obliged and a week later, handwritten notes arrived from all of the Team, including Stephen Fry, Tim Brooke-Taylor, Graeme Garden, Humphrey Littleton and, of course, Barry himself.

Needless to say, I'm Sorry I Haven't a Clue remains a firm favourite after all these years!

P.S. Thank you!

These three stories are great examples of those 'little things' that don't take much to give – but mean so much to receive.

Simple acts of your own kindness can make a huge difference in other people's lives.

It would have been easy for those involved to have become wound up in their own busy lives and to forget the commitments they made.

But they didn't.

They went out of their way, even if for just a few minutes, to make a positive impact on someone else's life – someone they didn't even know.

A huge and heartfelt THANK YOU to all concerned!

P.P.S If they can do it...

...So can you!

Take a few moments now to think about people in your own community – or perhaps further afield.

What can YOU do and who can YOU help in simple ways to make a difference to *their* lives.

How can YOU become a REMARKABLE Stranger?

And finally...

In the preceding pages and exercises, you've probably learned a lot...and learned a lot more about yourself!

It's a great starting point.

However, it's what you do <u>from now on</u> that REALLY matters and writing everything down is the first part of making things happen.

So, here's your last 'exercise'.

It's a simple one, to get you started on what's needed to create your own REMARKABLE future.

**Based on what you've learned from this book,
What is THE MOST IMPORTANT THING for
you to do <u>RIGHT NOW – as soon as you put this
book down -</u> to start creating your own
REMARKABLE Life?**

Take a moment to think about this and then write it down.

Make a real commitment to yourself to do this thing.

Then, say your commitment out loud – and MEAN it!

Then start DOING it!

Congratulations!

Your future SUCCESS lies ahead of you, much clearer than ever before. It's over to you to make it happen.

**Here's to your SUCCESSFUL FUTURE
and a new REMARKABLE YOU!**